Quilling Shapes

Look at all the shapes you can make with simple strips of paper!

Small Waves. Loose scrolls made with 3" strips.

Large Waves. Loose scrolls made with 6" strips.

Small Fish Head. Teardrop made with 6" strip. **Small Fish Tail.** Bunny ear made with 4" strip.

Large Fish Head. Teardrop made with 9" strip. **Large Fish Tail.** Bunny ear made with 6" strip.

Seaweed. Twist quilling paper and glue.

Tiny Heart. Open heart made with 3" strip.

Small Heart. Open heart made with 4" strip.

Large Heart. Open heart made with 5" strip.

Flower. ⅝" flower punch. Loose scroll stem made with 3" strip. Grape roll (see page 4) center made with 1" strip.

Basic Steps

Quilling comes in and ⅜"

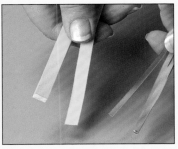

1. Punch flowers from cardstock and handcut leaves from quilling paper.

2. Choose width of quilling paper you wish to use.

3. Insert quilling paper in quilling tool.

4. Twist tool to roll quilling paper.

5. Remove paper and pinch sides to shape.

6. Glue quilled shapes on paper.

Basic Quilling Shapes

Tight Circle. Tightly roll the paper strip on a quilling tool. After rolling the paper, glue the loose end and remove the strip from the tool.

Loose Circle. Gently roll the paper strip on the quilling tool. Remove the strip from the tool and set it aside to loosen to the desired size. Glue loose end.

Teardrop. Roll a loose circle and glue end. Pinch one side of circle into a teardrop.

Marquise. Roll a loose circle and glue end. See the circle as a clock and pinch opposite sides at 3 o'clock and 9 o'clock to shape the marquise.

Shaped Marquise. Make a marquise and shape ends by pushing one end down and the other end up.

Bunny Ear. Roll a loose circle and glue end. See the circle as a clock, pinch at 10 o'clock and 2 o'clock and make a curved indentation at the top.

Crescent. Roll a loose circle and glue end. See the circle as a clock, pinch at 8 o'clock and 4 o'clock and shape the middle to form a crescent.

Half Circle. Roll a loose circle and glue end. See the circle as a clock, pinch at 7 o'clock and 5 o'clock and pull tight to flatten one side of the circle.

Square. Roll a loose circle and glue end. Pinch into a marquise, then turn and pinch the opposite sides. Rectangles are similar with the second pinch made closer to first pinch.

Triangle. Roll a loose circle and glue end. Pinch circle in 3 places and use your finger to form the triangle.

Scrolls

Loose Scroll. Roll one end and leave the other end straight.

Open Heart. Fold the paper strip in half and roll each end toward the center.

V Scroll. Fold the paper strip in half and roll each end toward the outside.

C Scroll. Roll both ends of the paper strip toward the center. This is similar to the open heart except the paper strip is not folded in half.

S Scroll. Roll one end of the quilling paper to the center. Turn the paper over and roll the other end to the center.

Flag. Fold the paper strip in half. Roll both ends at the same time.

Other Quilling Techniques

Grape Roll. Make a tight circle and glue the end. Gently push the center up to create a dome effect. Apply a thin layer of glue inside so the roll will retain its shape.

Spiral. Position the paper strip on the tapered needle tool near the handle and at an angle. Roll the strip tightly, spiraling down the tool. This will allow the spiral to slide off the tool's point.

Pompom. To begin, fringe quilling paper with a pair of scissors or a fringing tool. The most common widths of quilling paper to fringe are $1/4$" and $3/8$". Roll the fringed paper into a tight circle, glue the loose end and remove from the tool.

Fringed Flower. To begin, fringe $1/4$" or $3/8$" paper with a pair of scissors or fringing tool. Glue $1/8$" paper to the end of the fringed piece. Roll $1/8$" paper until it reaches the fringed piece and continue rolling until you have a tight circle. Glue the loose end and remove from tool. Use your fingers to open the flower.

Swirl Flowers

1. With water pen make a really wet circle on the cardstock and tear out. Wet a spiral.

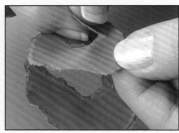

2. Tear out the spiral.

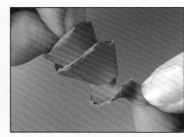

3. Starting from the outside end, roll until you reach the center to make spiral. Glue to secure.

Husking

Husking is made by wrapping quilling paper around pins arranged in a straight line on paper. Graph paper or measured markings are used to achieve uniform distance, but differing widths can be used to make unusual patterns.

Make as many loops as the pattern or your imagination require. A drop of glue at the end of each overlap will secure the paper.

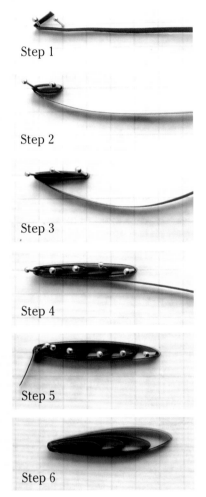

Step 1

Step 2

Step 3

Step 4

Step 5

Step 6

Large Shapes for 'Quick Quilling'

Loose Scrolls - Use to make waves, sun rays and beards.

Teardrops - Use to make wings, flowers and balloons.

Huskings - Use to make trim, fire and tree branches.

Marquise Rolls - Use for flowers, wheels and accents.

Tight Roll - Use to make flowers, insect bodies, flower centers, buttons and gumballs.

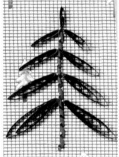

V Scroll Rolls - Use for hearts and antennae.

Layered Flowers

1. Punch balloons. Roll one balloon into funnel shape with slotted tool .

2. Curl 4 balloons from side to side, cut halfway up center. Glue first piece inside open flap of funnel. Glue remaining pieces inside flap of previous piece.

3. Curl top edges of 6 to 8 balloons, cut halfway up center and glue in place.

4. Curl petals on both sides of 10 to 12 balloons, cut halfway up center and glue in place.

5. Let dry, turn over and cut off excess paper so flower will lie flat.

Santa
MATERIALS: *Bazzill Basics* cardstock (White, Black, Flesh) • *Paper Patch* Burgundy paper • *Windows of Time* Santa paper piecing pattern • 1/8" White quilling paper • White gel pen • Black pen

by Katrina Hogan

Tree - MATERIALS: *Bazzill Basics* cardstock (Brown, 1/4" x 2 1/2" strips of Green)

Ladybug
MATERIALS: 1/8" and 1/4" quilling paper (True Red, Black)

FIR TREE

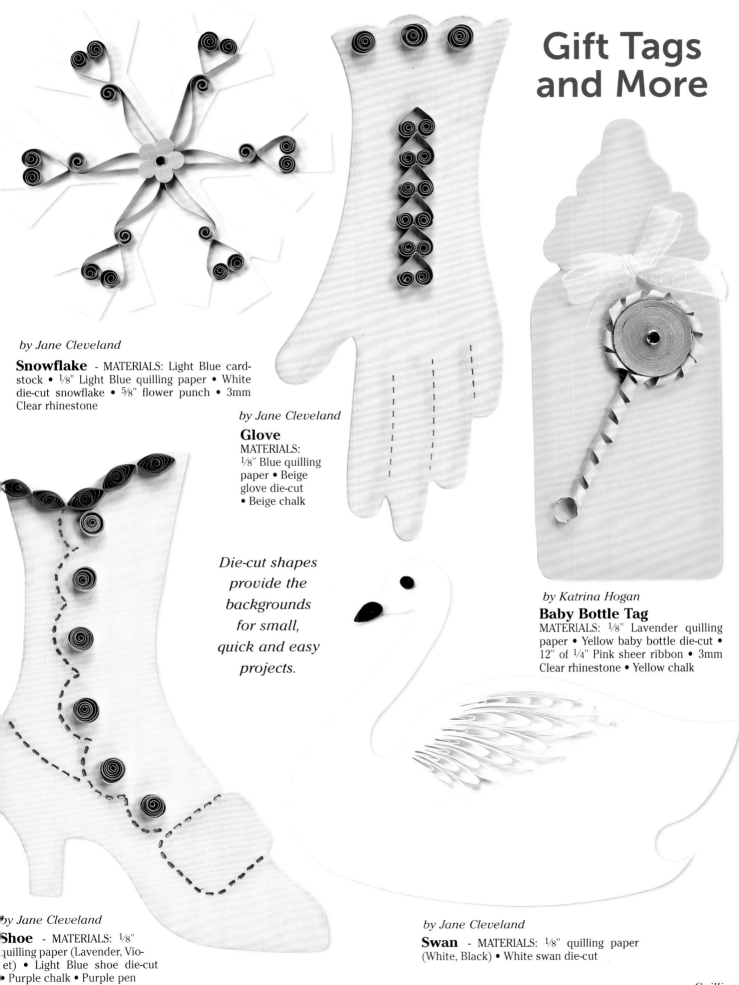

Gift Tags and More

by Jane Cleveland

Snowflake - MATERIALS: Light Blue cardstock • 1/8" Light Blue quilling paper • White die-cut snowflake • 5/8" flower punch • 3mm Clear rhinestone

by Jane Cleveland

Glove
MATERIALS:
1/8" Blue quilling paper • Beige glove die-cut • Beige chalk

Die-cut shapes provide the backgrounds for small, quick and easy projects.

by Katrina Hogan

Baby Bottle Tag
MATERIALS: 1/8" Lavender quilling paper • Yellow baby bottle die-cut • 12" of 1/4" Pink sheer ribbon • 3mm Clear rhinestone • Yellow chalk

by Jane Cleveland

Shoe - MATERIALS: 1/8" quilling paper (Lavender, Violet) • Light Blue shoe die-cut • Purple chalk • Purple pen

by Jane Cleveland

Swan - MATERIALS: 1/8" quilling paper (White, Black) • White swan die-cut

Shirt & Pants Card
MATERIALS: *Bazzill* cardstock (8" x 12" piece of Navy Blue stripe, Red) • Print paper (*Design Originals* stars and stripes on White, denim) • Quilling paper (⅛" White and Cadet Blue, ⅜" Holiday Green) • 18" of ¼" Gold sheer ribbon • 4 Red 3mm and 4 Clear 4mm rhinestones • Punches (⅝" flower, ⅛" circle) • Deckle scissors

Skirt & Stripe Blouse Card
MATERIALS: *Bazzill Basics* cardstock (6" x 8" piece of Dark Red, Navy Blue) • Paper (star stripe, Turquoise) • Quilling paper (⅛" White, ⅜" Holiday Green) • ⅝" flower punch • 3 Blue 3mm rhinestones • Deckle scissors

Skirt & Heart Blouse Card
MATERIALS: *Bazzill* cardstock (6" x 8" piece of White, Red) • Print paper (heart, denim) • Quilling paper (⅛" Light Blue and Soft Yellow, ⅜" Holiday Green) • ⅝" flower punch • 3 Red 3mm rhinestones • Deckle scissors

Blouse or Shirt – with No Front Seam

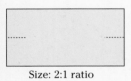

Size: 2:1 ratio

1. Cut a 3" x 6" rectangle of paper. With colored side up, pinch center of each short end.

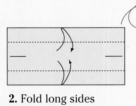

2. Fold long sides to center, crease and unfold.

3. With white up, fold down top edge equal to side fold width. **4.** Fold the cut edge up to folded edge, crease and unfold.

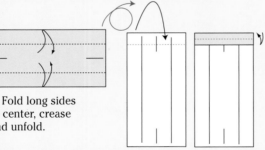

1/3
1/3
1/3

5. Fold bottom edge up ⅓ the height of figure. Be accurate.

6. Unfold so top edge is cut edge again. Turn project over.

7. Fold long sides in to meet at center along existing creases.

8. Lift loose corners at bottom center and make slanted folds.

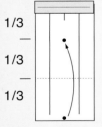

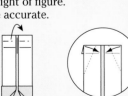

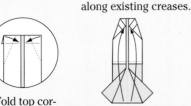

9. Fold top edge to back on top crease.

10. Fold top corners down to meet at intersection of horizontal crease and center line.

11. Lift bottom edge and slide it under points of collar. Crease at new bottom edge.

12. The completed blouse/shirt with opening at bottom where pant or skirt may be inserted. For shirt, fold bottom sides back at an angle.

Shirt with Front Seam

1. Cut a 3" x 3" square of paper. Fold square in half, unfold.

2. Fold each half in half again to meet at center.

3. To find center, fold in half top to bottom, unfold.

4. Fold bottom inside right and left corners

5. Fold bottom half back to meet top edge.

6. Fold top center right and left corners down to form collar.

7. Fold tip of shoulders back to round them off.

8. Optional: Fold sides diagonally form taper.

Cuff Option: To make sleeve cuff and center button placket, make a small vertical fold along right and left edge of square paper before folding shirt.

9. Finished sh

Pleated Skirt

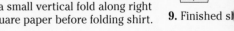

1. Cut a 2" x 6" strip of paper. To make pleats the same size and to fold accurately, lightly draw guidelines on the back of paper with a pencil and ruler.

2. Fold paper back and forth to crease along each line.

3. Shape accord folds into a skirt. Stre lower end to desi fullness and upper to match width of tom of shirt.

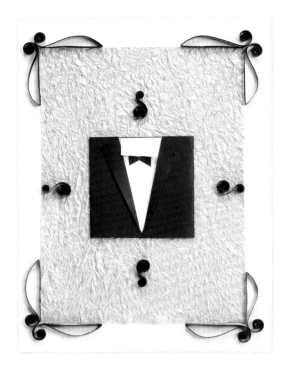

Tuxedo - MATERIALS: *Bazzill Basics* cardstock (5" x 6" piece of White stripe , Black, White stripe for shirt) • Silver crinkle paper • ⅛" Black quilling paper

Pants

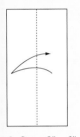 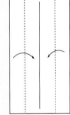  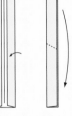

1. Cut a 3" x 6" rectangle of paper. With white side up, fold in half lengthwise. Crease and unfold.

2. Fold each half in half lengthwise to meet at center.

3. Fold in half again along existing crease.

4. Fold diagonally in half to make pants.

5. Slide pants into opening at bottom of shirt.

Tuxedo

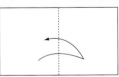 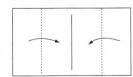

1. Cut 4" x 10" pieces of black cardstock and white cardstock. Fold in half vertically, unfold.

2. Fold left and right sides in half to meet center fold line.

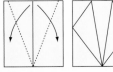 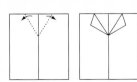

3. For coat, fold top right center corner diagonally out to right side. Repeat on left side. Tuck white shirt inside tuxedo coat.

4. For tux shirt, fold top right center corner diagonally out to the right to meet the edge of the tux lapel. Repeat on left side.

Matching Skirt & Blouse - MATERIALS: *Bazzill Basics* cardstock (6" x 7" piece of Dark Red, White) • Heart plaid print paper • Quilling paper (⅛" Soft Yellow and Green, ⅜" Ivory and Seafoam Green) • 3mm rhinestones (3 Red, 3 Clear, 3 Blue) • Deckle scissors

Quilling and Clothing

Combine paper folding and quilling to make a page or card filled with color and texture.

by Jane Cleveland

Western Shirt & Pants
MATERIALS: *Bazzill Basics* cardstock (8" x 12" piece of Seafoam Green, Black, White) • Paper (Silver, Black check) • ⅛" Black quilling paper • 18" of ¼" White sheer ribbon • 3 Black 3mm rhinestones • ⅛" circle punch • Deckle scissors
TIP: Make string tie with a narrow piece of quilling paper.

Fanciful Borders

Borders are easy, fun and fabulous when you combine quilled designs with punched and cut out shapes.

by Laura Greg

Joy - MATERIALS: White *Bazzill Basics* cardstock • Metallic Gold paper • ⅛" Holiday Green quilling paper • Red paper twist • 1¾" *Dayco* Red letter die-cuts • 4 Metallic Gold photo corners

by Jane Clevela

Flower Border - MATERIALS: *Bazzill Basics* cardstock (Lavender, White, Pink) • Quilling paper (⅛" Pale Green and Soft Yellow, ⅜" Pale Green, Yellow and Violet) • 3mm rhinestones (4 Pink, 4 Clear) • ⅝" flower punch

by Jane Clevela

Friends - MATERIALS: Red *Bazzill Basics* cardstock • ⅛" White quilling paper • *Daisy D's* heart paper • 1¾" letter die-cuts

by Laura Gregory

Home
MATERIALS: *Wubie* Brick print paper • ⅛" Brown quilling paper • *Dayco* Cream 1½" die-cut letters

Flower
MATERIALS: *Bazzill Basics* card-stock (Tan, Green) • ⅜" quilling paper (White, Bright Yellow, Holiday Green) • *Stampin' Up* ivy stamp • Green ink pad

White Flower Border
MATERIALS: *Bazzill Basics* card-stock (White, Light Blue) • Quilling paper (⅛" White, ⅜" White) • 6 Clear 2 mm rhinestones • ⅝" flower punch

Love Border
MATERIALS: Heart print paper • Quilling paper (⅛" White, ⅛" Red) • *Dayco* Red heart and 1¾" letter die-cuts • White chalk

by Katrina Hogan   by Jane Cleveland   by Laura Gregory

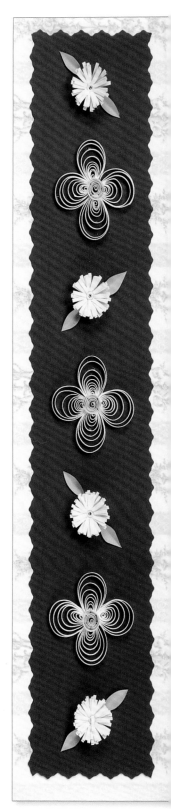

by Jane Cleveland

Tan Border
MATERIALS: *Bazzill* cardstock (Tan, Rust) • *Over the Moon Press* print paper • Quilling paper (1/8" Green, Brown, Burgundy and Deep Rose, 3/8" Burgundy and Gold) • 1/2" maple leaf punch

by Katrina Hogan

Balloon Border
MATERIALS: Bright Yellow *Bazzill* cardstock • *EK Success* landscape paper • 1/8" quilling paper (Violet, True Red, Yellow, Black)

by Jane Cleveland

Green Border
MATERIALS: *Bazzill* cardstock (Rust, Light Green) • Quilling paper (1/8" Periwinkle Blue, Yellow, Magenta, Cadet Blue, Holiday Green and Rust, 3/8" Holiday Green) • Miniature rake and seed packet • Gardening stickers • Decorative scissors

by Jane Cleveland

Burgundy Border
MATERIALS: *Bazzill* Burgundy cardstock • *Anna Griffin* print paper • Quilling paper (1/8" White and Soft Yellow, 3/8" Flesh and Seafoam Green) • Decorative scissors
Tip - See flower & leaf on page

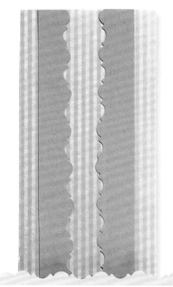

Fanciful Borders

Delicate little border designs are a snap with quilled flowers, punched shapes and a few embellishments.

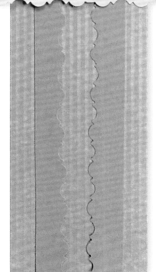

by Jane Cleveland

Pink Border

MATERIALS: *Bazzill* cardstock (Pink, Blue, Yellow) • Quilling paper (1/8" Meadow Green and Yellow, 3/8" Meadow Green, Pale Pink and Cadet Blue) • 4 Pink 3mm rhinestones • 5/8" flower punch • Decorative scissors

by Laura Gregory, quilling by Jane Cleveland

Baby Buggy Border

MATERIALS: *Bazzill* cardstock (Pink, White, Light Blue) • *Worldwin* Silver pin stripe paper • 1/8" quilling paper (White, Silver Grey, Pink, Light Blue) • 8" of 1/8" Light Blue satin ribbon • Pop dots • Decorative scissors

TIPS: To weave buggy body, tape strips of Pink quilling paper side by side. Weave with alternating Blue and White strips. Glue on White cardstock and cut out buggy shape.

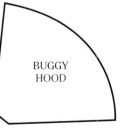

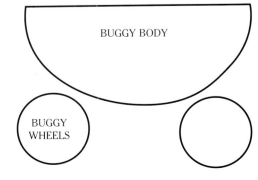

BUGGY HOOD

BUGGY BODY

BUGGY WHEELS

Faith is the substance of
things hoped for,
the evidence of things
not seen.
Hebrews 11:1

Tag,
You're It!

by Jane Cleveland

Gold Tag - MATERIALS: Gold tag die-cut • Quilling paper (⅛" Pale Green and Soft Yellow, ⅜" Turquoise and Pale Green) • 3 Yellow 3mm rhinestones • Computer generated message

Party!

Date: _____

Time: _____

Place: _____

by Laura Gregory

Party Tag & Envelope - MATERIALS: 'Happy Birthday' print paper • Green tag die-cut • ⅛" quilling paper (Yellow, Black) • ¼" Red curling ribbon • Computer generated message

by Jane Cleveland

Yellow Flower Tag - MATERIALS: Yellow die-cut tag • Quilling paper (⅛" Rust, Ivory and Green, ⅜" Rust and Green)

by Jane Cleveland

Blue Tag - MATERIALS: Blue tag die-cut • ⅛" White quilling paper

Thank You Tag - MATERIALS: Turquoise cardstock • Pink tag die-cut • Quilling paper (⅛" Yellow and Turquoise, ⅜" Soft Green) • ½" Black letter stickers • 2 Clear 3mm rhinestones

THANK
YOU

by Jane Cleveland

Special Occasion Tags

Decorated tags are perfect for invitations, greeting cards and thank you notes.

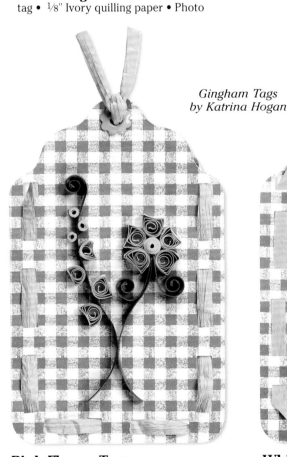

by Laura Gregory

Birthday Tag - MATERIALS: Yellow tag die-cut • ⅛" quilling paper (Turquoise, Black) • Red 'Happy Birthday' sticker

by Laura Gregory

Photo Tag - MATERIALS: Dark Blue die-cut tag • ⅛" Ivory quilling paper • Photo

Gingham Tags by Katrina Hogan

Pink Flower Tag
MATERIALS: Blue plaid paper • ⅛" quilling paper (Pink, Yellow, Green) • Beige paper twist • Yellow flower eyelet • Eyelet setter • Punches (⅛" circle, ³⁄₁₆" square)

White Flower Tag
MATERIALS: Blue plaid paper • ⅛" quilling paper (White, Gold, Green) • Golden paper twist • Yellow flower eyelet • Eyelet setter • Punches (⅛" circle, ³⁄₁₆" square)

Large Pink Flower Tag
MATERIALS: Blue plaid paper • ⅛" quilling paper (Pink, Bright Yellow, Green) • Golden paper twist • Yellow flower eyelet • Eyelet setter • Punches (⅛" circle, ³⁄₁₆" square)

by Jane Cleveland

Green Butterfly
MATERIALS: Green butterfly die-cut • ⅛" quilling paper (Black, Yellow, Turquoise) • 1" long Black paper bead

Ladybug - MATERIALS: Red ladybug die-cut • ⅛" Black quilling paper

by Laura Gregory

Aqua Butterfly
MATERIALS: ⅛" quilling paper (Black, Orange, Aqua) • ½" long Black paper bead

by Jane Cleveland

by Katrina Hogan

Red Flower
MATERIALS: ¼" parchment quilling paper (Red, Green) • 10mm Clear rhinestone

by Katrina Hogan

Cheerleader - MATERIALS: *Paperkins* doll and clothes die-cuts • ⅛" White quilling paper • 2 Black 6mm pompoms • ½" Black letter sticker

by Jane Cleveland
Stocking - MATERIALS: Red and White stocking die-cuts • ⅛" quilling paper (White, Holiday Green, Yellow, True Red) • Black pen

by Laura Gregory
Mitten - MATERIALS: Cardstock (Yellow, Violet) • Blue mitten die-cut • ⅛" quilling paper (True Red, Yellow, Violet) • Black pen

Die-Cuts

Accent die-cuts or create dimensional shapes with quilling for spectacular results!

by Jane Cleveland
Corn
MATERIALS: Green corn die-cut • ⅛" Gold quilling paper • Natural paper twist

by Laura Gregory
Christmas Tree
MATERIALS: Green tree die-cut • ⅛" quilling paper (Gold, True Red, White) • Dark Green fiber • Red bow

by Jane Cleveland
Gumball Machine - MATERIALS: Green gumball machine die-cut • ⅛" quilling paper (White, Yellow, True Red, Black, Meadow Green, Violet, Cadet Blue)

Borders and More Borders

You can make a border for every season or event with quilled designs and a few simple accents.

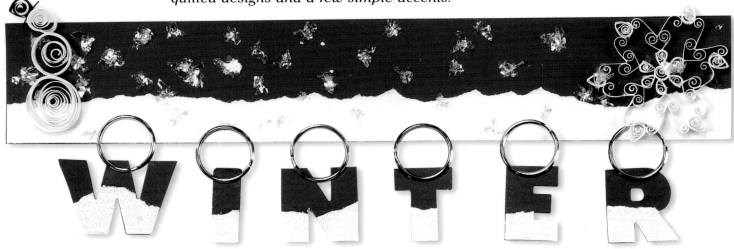

by Katrina Hogan and Laura Gregory

Winter Border - MATERIALS: *Bazzill Basics* cardstock (Blue, White) • ⅛" quilling paper (White, Black) • *Sizzix* 1¼" Blue and White letter die-cuts • *ZBarten* Party ice and Iridescent glitter • 6 Silver 1" split rings

by Ruth Ann Warwick

Thanksgiving Border - MATERIALS: *Bazzill Basics* cardstock (Dark Green, Ivory) • ⅛" quilling paper (Gold, Yellow, Orange, True Red) • Paperkins doll and clothes die-cuts • Six assorted Beige buttons • Foam tape • Green and Brown pens

by Ruth Ann Warwick, quilling by Jane Cleveland

Duck Border - MATERIALS: Bazzill Basics cardstock (Blue, Brown, Dark Brown) • ⅛" quilling paper (Orange, Yellow) • Green grass die cut • Foam tape • Brown and Green chalk